The Importance of Being Algy

Praise for Algy Cluff's previous books

Get On With It

'At seventy-six, he reflects in this memoir on a blissful-sounding life at home and abroad – high jinks in the Army, languorous City luncheons primed by pink gins, drilling successfully for oil in the North Sea, mining diamonds in Africa and becoming friendly with such disparate figures as Margaret Thatcher and Zimbabwe's notorious President Robert Mugabe...

Enjoyably gossipy, *Get On With It* also contains valuable insights into business and political life... Appropriately, playwright Sir Tom Stoppard suggests his next book should be called *The Importance Of Being Algy*.'

—*Daily Mail*

'... one of the few books I'd read which I wished longer...'

—Charles Moore, *The Spectator*

'When he was a small boy at boarding school in the 1940s, Algy Cluff's imagination was captivated by hectic tales of derring-do in the novels of John Buchan. He resolved then to actualise this imaginary world of Clubland heroes. For the past half-century he has been, as this

rattling, full-throttled, red-blooded memoir shows, a strenuous, venturesome capitalist in Richard Hannay's mould.'
—Richard Davenport-Hines, *TLS*

'A cross-pollination of James Bond and Indiana Jones, with an eye for adventure and a real talent for entrepreneurship.'
—*KCW Today*

Unsung Heroes
'… a splendid book…'
—*The Times*

'I warmly recommend it… Although Algy's own life has been extremely active and successful, his greatest gift is for describing, affectionately, lives of which this could not be said.'
—Charles Moore, *The Spectator*

The Importance of Being Algy

Algy Cluff

Cluff & Sons

The Ian Fleming chapter is adapted from an article originally written for *The Oldie*. Reproduced by kind permission.

Every reasonable effort has been made to trace copyright holders of material reproduced in this book, but if any have been inadvertently overlooked the publishers would be glad to hear from them.

Edited, designed and produced by Tandem Publishing
http://tandempublishing.yolasite.com

ISBN: 978-1-9168994-1-4

10 9 8 7 6 5 4 3 2 1

A CIP catalogue record for this book is available from the British Library.

Printed and bound in Great Britain by CPI Group (UK) Ltd, Croydon CR0 4YY.

To my three admirable and formidable sons,
Harry, Philip and Charlie, with a combined
height of twenty feet.

I'm grateful to Sir Tom Stoppard for
suggesting the title of this volume at a dinner
at The Other Club.

Also by Algy Cluff

Get On With It
Unsung Heroes
By the Way…
Off the Cluff

CONTENTS

Whither, O splendid ship, thy white sails
   crowding,
Leaning across the bosom of the urgent West

'A Passer-by', Robert Bridges

Foreword

Harry Mount

One of the delicious tales in this charming book recounts Algy Cluff's meeting with Ian Fleming in 1963.

There they were at Boodle's – Fleming, fifty-six, with only a year to live; Algy, twenty-three, in the flush of youth, in the Grenadier Guards. Fleming reveals his great regret: 'I wanted to be the Captain of the Royal St George's Golf Club.' That was the club, in Sandwich, that inspired the Royal St Mark's in *Goldfinger*.

In fact, Fleming was about to become Captain the following year when he dropped dead after a heart attack on the 18th green.

That is, in itself, a wonderfully tragic story. But Algy adds a coda that's tragicomic gold.

Algy, with customary generosity, wanted to add a signed picture of Fleming to complement the golf club's collection of photographs of club captains. No, came the answer. Fleming 'never quite made it'. And so Fleming – the most dashing, famous writer to swing a three iron at

Royal St George's – was denied his spot on the wall.

The story encapsulates Algy's gift for observation and storytelling. It also shows how unique he is. Some clubmen might remember a story from sixty years ago. Very few would be generous enough to give away such a rare picture to their golf club. Only Algy would do both – and see the comic value in Fleming's rejection from the photograph gallery ('mostly Old Etonian stockbrokers') at St George's.

Sadly, Ian Fleming met Algy only late in life. Otherwise, you could make a very convincing case for Algy being the model for James Bond: tall, slim, good-looking, impeccably tailored, with a dashing record in the armed forces – plus a gift for funny one-liners.

And, dare I say it, there were a fair few Bond Girls – or Cluff Girls – on the scene before Algy met his match in Blondel, his planet-brained, beautiful wife.

Every turn in Algy's life has produced unique contradictions. He left the Grenadier Guards and, a few years later, struck black gold as one of the first buccaneering oilmen in the North Sea.

But how many oilmen are P. G. Wodehouse devotees, like Algy? And how many oilmen love magazines so much that they buy an actual magazine itself – in Algy's case, the *Spectator*?

And how many Grenadier Guards officers would return to the Officers' Mess at St James's Palace and have the eye to notice that 'the oil portraits of Queen Victoria and Lord Kitchener remained as they were, although a rather louche screen of Edwardian high jinks has disappeared'?

With this rare combination of commercialacumen,militaryderring-doandman-of-letters curiosity, Algy has sent back these more-ish reports from the worlds of business, the Army, politics and a daring new venture in his 80s: White Cliffs of Dover Sparkling Wine.

Only Algy would have noticed Lord Lucan – some time before he murdered the family nanny – training an unfortunate dog in Eaton Square:

'This he did by administering electric shocks to the animal via a console to a collar around the animal's neck which used to involuntarily leap one foot into the air, as Lucan, in Bond-villain style, sought to convince the poor animal to conform to his instructions. One short step from torturing your dog to murdering your nanny, I should have realised.'

Algy has inwardly absorbed the funniest

aspects of P. G. Wodehouse's prose style. In the case of Mark Birley, the founder and owner of Annabel's nightclub, 'his conversation had a terse and witty economy in which small talk played no part. That is not to say that his conversation was on a higher plane...

'His economy of words was amusingly described to me by a New York socialite and beauty, Caroline Cushing. She spent a week staying with Mark in his Pelham Crescent house, during which the only words he addressed to her were "you are standing in front of the set".'

Algy is the gentlest of souls but, like all the best Englishmen, he is also a great tease and delights in being teased. Thus this passage on the late Lord Reay:

'Hugh Reay was experiencing a challenging period in his life which rendered him aloof, silent (almost Trappist), leading me to bestow on him the sobriquet "Chatty"!

'I recall seeing Hugh one day sitting at his desk in his enormous house in Wilton Crescent. He was staring at a blank piece of paper. "What are you doing Hugh?" I enquired. "I am working on my approach," was his enigmatic response.'

That response, with its echoes of the golf links, is worthy of the Master himself – P. G. Wodehouse.

Algy is a rare, well-qualified correspondent from Planet Plutocrat. He is neither bitter, as so many visitors to that planet are, nor is he oleaginous about its residents.

Instead, he is objective and full of gripping information. I didn't know that points on credit cards and air miles don't attract tax. That's one of the reasons tycoons love business travel so much.

And yet – in his disarming way – Algy then goes on to say that, despite this perk, 'So much of business travel is totally unnecessary that there should be another column in reports and accounts revealing the travel costs (including class) of the executives.'

He proceeds to tell the instructive story of Sir Alfred Chester Beatty (1875–1968), the King of Copper, who made a fortune out of African metal, while never straying further from Kensington Palace Gardens than to the City of London – 'admittedly in the back of a huge Rolls-Royce'.

What characters Algy has met along the way in his astounding life. What joy P. G. would have had to read Algy on Lord Stanley: 'He inherited a large fortune which was greatly diminished by two sets of death duties, by his zest for life and for women, including five marriages – a record even for a member of White's.'

If only P. G. Wodehouse had met Algy, the Master could have been even funnier.

THE IMPORTANCE OF BEING ALGY

White Cliffs of Dover
Sparkling Wine

OUR HOUSE STANDS three hundred feet above sea level on a promontory on top of the White Cliffs of Dover. Behind it, bisected by an Anglo-Saxon road 2,000 years old, there exists a field of about nine acres that I was able to acquire from a local farmer. That was twenty-five years ago. There it sat, with the grass being cut by the same farmer year after year.

Then, on a trip to visit General de Gaulle's house at Colombey-les-Deux-Églises with two of my sons, Philip and Charlie, we entered

Champagne country and, whilst the two boys were engaged in whatever was emanating from their headphones, I set to musing on whether planting a vineyard could be the solution to those fallow acres. Charlie Cluff, at the time eighteen years old and 6 foot 8 inches tall, slept soundly through most of the drive from Calais. Disaster nearly occurred when I stopped for fuel, had a minor nervous breakdown paying for it, returned to the car and was about to rejoin the motorway when Philip shouted 'Stop, Charlie's gone for a walk!' Far from being asleep, he had uncoiled his frame and, whilst rolling a cigarette, was stung by a wasp, while I was seconds away from abandoning him.

Happily, together we arrived at a rather self-important hotel in Colombey and enjoyed an interesting visit to the General's house the following morning, where we were duly impressed by the modesty and austerity of the great man's quarters, before moving to stay with the Berry family (William, his wife Eleanor and his brother Alexander, sons of my close friend Nicholas who alas died in 2016) at Sologne near Orléans. All the while my brain was focused on Champagne. My father had run a wine shipping business and I had always regretted the sale of the business (prompted by my hapless judgement that trade was infra-dig). Alcohol was accordingly in my blood in more ways than one.

Our epic trip was planned to conclude with a night in Le Touquet before a leisurely ferry crossing the following morning. We arrived tired out at the Westminster Hotel, where they denied any knowledge of our existence, so we returned to the car for a frantic drive to Calais where we managed to connect with the last ferry and thankfully spent the night in our own beds on the White Cliffs. The following day I studied my father's wine library (he was a good friend of legendary wine bore André Simon) and I quickly realised that there were certain arguments in favour of a new sparkling wine vineyard. Two of which: the geology being ad idem with Épernay, and the location being maritime, where the mortal enemy of young vines, frost, is virtually unknown. This persuaded me to dismiss the disadvantages – primarily the wind from the east. Of course, the other advantage was that I already owned the land.

So, my wife and I resolved to take the plunge. My eldest son Harry is friendly with the son of John Knight, a low-key but highly effective oilman who was then the most senior non-Norwegian in Statoil. It transpired that he had taken the plunge five years earlier and has a flourishing vineyard near Guildford. John introduced me to his viticulturist, and then a team of Germans duly materialised and planted 4,000 vines of the Pinot Noir grape. They were followed by some indomitable Romanians who installed the steel frames to which the vines attach themselves in due course. So, we were off. To say we were neophytes in this world would be an understatement, but somehow my wife, of Caribbean farming stock, together with our admirable ex-Gurkha Sergeant Major Chau Gurung, have weeded, strimmed and generally cared for our vines.

It is our intention to do everything ourselves and we are blessed because during the last war the whole of the White Cliffs of Dover, including our house and garden, had been taken over by the Army, and they installed mammoth ammunition bunkers. They are indestructible and, apart from a hilarious period during which the police convinced themselves that I was hiding Lord Lucan within, have really proved of no practical use. Now, however, they come into their own as warehouses to store the bottles. As to the taste, Rob Saunders declared last year that he rates it 11 out of 10, with an invigorating salty flavour derived from the east wind, which we had feared so much. 2022 was a year of drought and record temperatures in southern England. The climate factor was compounded by my inability to source any casual labour at all, although in truth fewer than half the 4,000 vines exhibited a full crop of grapes, which gave us some concern.

Our resolve, however, was significantly strengthened by our Kentish neighbours and vineyard owners, Lorna Wilks and George Jessel, and by expert advice from Vine Care in Brighton. So, we are committed to investing more time and a modest amount of money to yield a crop in 2023. As I write I notice an interview in the *Financial Times* with a leading light in the Champagne industry who contends that English Sparkling Wine will never rival the French variety as the soil will never compare to that of Épernay. So, I look forward to sending him a bottle of our 'White Cliffs of Dover Sparkling Wine – Vera Lynn', vintage 2023!

Ian Fleming

I ENJOYED ATTENDING not one but two sixtieth anniversary dinners to mark the launch of the first James Bond film, *Dr No*. They were held at the Special Forces Club in London and at the Swedish Embassy. The Swedish Ambassador, Mikaela Kumlin Granit, is not only a Bond fan but would also well qualify as a Bond Girl!

These occasions were choreographed by a remarkable individual who is writing 007's biography – Paul Beaver. He uniquely holds the rank of Group Captain and Lieutenant

Colonel and is a renowned aircraft historian, having written seventy-five books.

We had a spirited discussion about where Bond had been educated, where he had served in the last war and where the next film was to be located. Sweden was the favoured choice, with a historical plot revolving around denial of Nazi access to iron ore deposits an obvious subject. We also wondered whether it was any longer necessary for Bond to be heterosexual or even English!

Attendance at these events led me to realise that, apart from a member of the Fleming family (James, his nephew and also a distinguished author), I was the only participant who had actually met Fleming.

This occurred in 1963 at Fleming's much-loved and much-used club, Boodle's. It was to Boodle's that he repaired to avoid the high-octane society which infested (as he saw it) his house in Victoria Square, invited there by his wife Ann. Blades – the locale of the Drax–Bond card contest in *Moonraker* – was obviously based on Boodle's. I have recently taken Paul Beaver to the club to show him the famous card room, still in active use.

One year in 1963, the year before Fleming died, aged only fifty-six, I found myself sitting next to him at a Boodle's dinner. He was charming and not at all intimidating to a youngster of twenty-three. I was in the Grenadier Guards at the time and about to be deployed to Cyprus.

During our chat, he revealed how tiresome he found the celebrity that claimed him. By then he had written most of the 007 books. He went on to say that sort of fame was not what he wanted in life.

So, I impudently said, 'Well, what *did* you want in life then?'

He replied, 'I wanted to be the Captain of the Royal St George's Golf Club.' The club, in Sandwich, inspired the Royal St Mark's in *Goldfinger*.

At this time, he was the Captain-Elect. Tragically, the following year, and before his elevation to Captain, he had a heart attack on the 18th green at Royal St George's and was taken to hospital in Canterbury. That was his final round.

Some twenty years later, having become a member of Royal St George's myself in 1972, a close friend of mine, Sir Patrick Sheehy, was himself appointed the Captain. Pat was a larger-than-life character – the Chairman of British American Tobacco. His intimidating appearance and growling manner terrified everyone.

In fact, this was a successful ace he adopted to facilitate his quest for the top job at BAT. In reality, he was a clever, kind and good man.

I had accumulated a number of original photographs of renowned golfers who had had an association with Royal St George's, including Bobby Sweeny (hanging in the club today) and C. J. Tolley. One was of Ian Fleming, wearing his Naval Commander's uniform. It was signed by Fleming.

I decided to donate these to the club and sent them to Pat. This, I thought, was pretty good of me. So, imagine my surprise when I received no acknowledgement. Worse, the Fleming photograph was then returned to me with a terse note from Pat to the effect that Fleming 'never quite made it'. In other words, he never actually became Captain.

So, in the club you can gaze at an array of photographs – mostly Old Etonian stockbrokers – who did 'make it', but no photograph of the club's most celebrated member by far.

To add further insult, my wife, during one of her periodic clean-outs of my hoard of books and photographs, included Fleming's signed photograph in a consignment gifted to the Oxfam shop.

Heaven knows where it is now!

The Peter Pan of Mayfair

ONE OF MY oldest friends is Billy Edgson who has, since 1969, successively been the doorman of the Clermont Club, of Annabel's, the nightclub beneath the Clermont at 44 Berkeley Square, then twenty-five years at Mark's Club in Charles Street followed by his current role at 5 Hertford Street.

In conversation with Billy recently, I ascertained that during all this time the palm for best-mannered aristocrat goes to Andrew, the 11th Duke of Devonshire. Conversely, the wooden spoon for the most obnoxious individual in any category: Sir Charles Clore. One evening Billy opened the door of Clore's Rolls and said, 'Good evening, Mr Clore.'

'*Sir* Charles to you and don't you forget it!' responded the tycoon, whose knighthood had been announced just that day in *The Times*; Billy's reading was confined to the racing papers. His overall hero was undoubtedly international backgammon champion and sportsman Philip Martyn, who could do no wrong.

Billy began his career as a delivery driver for a book publishing company, Constable Books, of Orange Square. Billy was responsible for the so-called West End run. This included an unofficial stop off – the Coach & Horses just off Hill Street in Mayfair, when it happened to be managed by Billy's uncle and aunt Jack and Anne Shimmon. One of the Coach & Horses regulars was Ian Maxwell-Scott, a heavily bespectacled and urbane old Etonian possessed of three interests: golf, darts and gambling.

The Coach & Horses boasted a dart board and was a two-minute walk from the Clermont Club where Ian, having lost his money at the Clermont tables, had converted from patron to employee, in fact as right-hand man to John Aspinall, the legendary proprietor and pioneer of gambling in the West End whilst it was illegal and later, by the late 1950s, legal. It transpired one evening, when Maxwell-Scott dropped into the Coach & Horses for his daily tipple, that he had a tale of woe – the Clermont stewards had decamped with the contents of the safe, and the insurance company now required the building to be permanently occupied. Maxwell-Scott promptly offered the Shimmons the job as stewards.

The Clermont had provided a permanent home for Aspinall's gambling parties when gaming was legalised in 1960. Previously, gambling on roulette and chemin de fer had been carried on at various private houses in Mayfair and Belgravia, and was generally left undisturbed even if illegal. Occasionally a zealous constable with inside information would conduct a raid, to the delight of the popular press as various ornaments of the aristocracy, somewhat dishevelled after a night in Gerald Road police station, were fined £20 by a magistrate the following morning. That was until one notable occasion when Aspinall elected to plead not guilty, and his barrister proceeded with great eloquence to advance the notion that in those rapidly changing times it was absurd to preserve such outdated laws. Aspinall was triumphantly acquitted.

Gaming immediately moved to a permanent base in Berkeley Square, and by way of commendation from his uncle Jack, Billy was granted an interview with Ian Maxwell-Scott for the job of doorman. When Billy entered Maxwell-Scott's office, the only paper on the desk was *Sporting Life*, and Maxwell-Scott appeared to be in a trance. He grumbled about Billy's youth and diminutive size but finally gave him the job (and four £10 notes). Within days Billy was on duty wearing a smart green quasi-military uniform and matching peaked cap. The first customer's car door which he made to open contained 'the richest man in the world' – and according to some also the meanest – Mr John Paul Getty.

It transpired that Billy's real boss was the head doorman, Charles Pearson, a distinguished-looking man who had previously been the head porter at White's. It also transpired that the 'Management' consisted of three people only: Aspinall, Ian Maxwell-Scott and Dan Meinertzhagen, both of the latter having come to grief at Aspinall's roulette tables.

Occasionally Lord Carnarvon put in an appearance, fulfilling his role as non-executive Chairman. The first car Billy parked at the Clermont Club belonged to an amazing City banker, Major Sir Trevor Dawson, all of six foot four, carnation in buttonhole and cigar in mouth. Billy got into a bit of a muddle parking the Major's Jaguar, but nothing compared to the muddle of the Major's financial affairs, which had involved him transferring huge amounts of clients' money to himself and which culminated in his suicide in his Eaton Square flat.

Sir Lloyd Dorfman recalls arriving at Mark's Club with his wife Sarah to be greeted by Billy with the news that a quadruped 'Dorfman' had that afternoon romped home in the 2.50 at Kempton Park. Sir Lloyd had never heard of his equine namesake, and his wife looked at him curiously, wondering whether he was maintaining a secret racing life. It was discovered the next day that Dorfman belonged to a celebrated Arab sheikh. When Dorfman had its next outing, Lloyd put £100 on the horse; Dorfman's jockey failed to remain on his mount and the horse failed to finish. That was the end of Sir Lloyd's racing interlude. It remains a mystery as to why the animal was so named.

***

Although there is no benefit to the house, Aspinall encouraged backgammon as a way of attracting natural gamblers. Prior to the opening of the Clermont, backgammon had mostly been played between 6pm and 8pm in all the St James's Street clubs, in particular at the St James's Club, which had a discrete room dedicated to it with six tables. It was a room peopled with the more louche characters of the day: Charles Jerdein (art dealer), Rupert Belville (professional gambler), Lord Lucan (ne'er-do-well), Michael Stoop (war hero), alongside more serious folk such as Lord (Joss) Pender (Chairman of Cable and Wireless), Ludovic Kennedy (broadcaster and husband of Moira Shearer) and David, Marquess of Milford Haven (war hero – at one point Chief Signals Officer of the Far Eastern Fleet). With the opening of the Clermont all the heavier gamblers abandoned the St James's and flocked there, only White's maintaining a lively backgammon coterie.

Transatlantic gamblers such as Claude Beer, Joe Dwek and Philip Martyn all congregated at the Clermont, rendering it the most sophisticated gaming club in the world. Billy has fond memories of two Clermont members who took their own lives and of a third, John Lucan, who probably did too. Robin Douglas-Home, nephew of Sir Alec, was a man about town and very popular with the ladies. His attractions were compounded by his talent as a jazz pianist, leading him to being offered a job by Aspinall playing the piano in the evening at the Clermont.

One weekend he was invited by Aspinall to stay at Howletts to meet the tigers and gorillas. At some point he asked Aspinall if he could photograph the animals together with the members of Aspinall's inner circle, who were staying the weekend. On Monday morning these photographs were reproduced in the *Daily Express*, to which they had clearly been sold by Douglas-Home. As recalled by Billy, Douglas-Home then appeared at the Clermont to collect his weekly stipend. Aspinall had just been advised of the treacherous conduct of his house pianist and demanded an axe with which to demolish the piano. Douglas-Home was warned by Pearson, the head doorman, to make himself scarce. Three months later he was dead by his own hand, having been ostracised by the Aspinall set.

Billy was much involved in the Lord Lucan affair, as indeed was I, having my house searched by 'the Lucan squad' from Gerald Road police station! At one stage, before the murder of nanny Sandra Rivett, Billy would take the two Lucan children to school in a DAF vehicle provided by his lordship, whose nights were so committed to playing for the house at the Clermont Club that he was incapable of fulfilling parental responsibilities.

Billy was as astounded as anyone else when the grisly and shockingly inept crime was committed, and has a view that Lucan had an accomplice. However, he will not reveal his identity. If there were such an accomplice, he must have taken off the moment it was evident that the wrong woman had been murdered. There is no doubt that Lucan turned up alone at the Maxwell-Scott residence in Sussex, the last person to see him alive being Ian Maxwell-Scott's wife. Billy does not have an opinion about what happened thereafter but leans to the view that Lucan's suicide was followed by the destruction of his corpse, duplicating whatever had been planned by Lucan to dispose of his wife's body. This does not, in my view, seem at all likely, particularly as he drove in Michael Stoop's borrowed car from the Maxwell-Scott house to the ferry terminal at Newhaven. Larger than life as indeed they were, it is beyond reasonable sense that the Clermont set would have allowed themselves to be complicit in an act of murder. The evidence supports the theory that Lucan committed suicide by launching himself from the deck of the Newhaven ferry into the freezing embrace of the English Channel.

After many years spent parking Rolls-Royces, Bentleys and Aston Martins in the vicinity of Mark Birley's eponymous Mark's Club whilst their owners caroused within, Billy achieved some celebrity within the local public houses for his matchless driving techniques. Some of the gentry who slaked their thirst alongside Billy had nefarious aspirations, which often required the services of a competent 'get away' driver, and inevitably Billy was subject to such suggestion. One day Billy, against his better judgement, agreed to drive the van containing the 'goods'. Alas the Constabulary intervened, and Billy was detained at Her Majesty's pleasure. Mark Birley, like his son always the most generous and loyal employer, and possessed of the kindest of hearts concealed within that intimidating exterior, was very fond of Billy, as indeed are so many of his club members, and he deemed Billy's aberration as more that of a sportsman than a rogue, and after Billy's sabbatical he seamlessly resumed his duties, navigating hundreds of thousands of pounds of machinery through the streets of Mayfair. To

Mark Birley, Billy also excelled at his job not only by reason of his handling of the vehicles but also his handling of their often-temperamental owners, for whom he remains a most popular and admired part of the Birley family empire.

Billy, now seventy-nine, continues to work as a doorman for Robin Birley at 5 Hertford Street. He is the Peter Pan of Mayfair, retaining today his charm and impish good looks.

***

I had a flat at 18 Eaton Square during the decline and collapse of the Lucan marriage. This was the section of Eaton Square set at a right angle to Lower Belgrave Street, the Lucan residence and murder scene. In the square there is a garden in which Lucan 'trained' some unfortunate dog (probably a Rhodesian Ridgeback); this he did by administering electric shocks to the animal via a console to a collar around the animal's neck, which used involuntarily to leap one foot into the air as Lucan, in Bond-villain style, sought to convince the poor animal to conform to his instructions. So objectionable was this that I was moved to intervene with my fellow clubman who, knowing of my friendship with his wife, was less than cordial. One short step from torturing your dog to murdering your nanny, I should have realised. It was about this time that a sensible judge refused custody of the children to their father, a judgment which although correct was the catalyst for the death of Sandra Rivett. It is worth recording that the two children whom Veronica Lucan brought up, notwithstanding the distressing background to their childhood, have both led successful and useful lives.

THE KING OF CLUBS

SHORTLY AFTER MARK Birley's eldest
son drowned off West Africa in 1986,
my Greek shipowner friend, Demetri
Marchessini, asked Mark and his daughter to
spend a week sailing from Corsica to Naples
on his family's motor yacht, *The Deineira*.
He also asked Colin Campbell and his wife,
together with Richard Soames and me, along
for the ride. A rather ill-suited group in the
circumstances, aggravated by Colin's excruciat-
ing cascade of jokes. There was instant sulphur
in the air between Campbell, who referred to

Mark, behind his back, as Lord Scattercash, and indeed Mark did nothing to conceal the wide disparity in their disposable incomes.

As a thank-you to Demetri, who was nothing if not a generous host, Mark brought on board what looked like a ten-gallon drum of caviar. This act of generosity had a surprising effect on our host for, instead of acknowledging the extraordinary gift, it was never mentioned. Instead of caviar with breakfast, lunch and dinner as we had anticipated, it was never seen or alluded to again. We even sent search parties into the boat's culinary regions, but they returned empty-handed. We finally concluded that Demetri, not the easiest of people, had judged the gift to be an insult to his hospitality and had consigned it to the bottom of the Mediterranean Sea.

To observe Mark at close quarters after such a devastating family tragedy was interesting. Mark never waffled, and in fact his conversation had a terse and witty economy in which small talk played no part. That is not to say that his conversation was on a higher plane, but it was disciplined and concise. He held fire until he had something pithy to say, which had the effect of rendering already nervous people, such as Colin Campbell, even more nervous. The less the inscrutable Mark said, the more the Campbells of this world blathered. The other interesting feature of this enigmatic man was his melancholia. According to his son, Robin, this can be attributed to his Irish ancestry. I, however, thought differently and detected a correlation between his increasing success and correspondingly increasing melancholia. As he was surrounded much of the time by genuflecting sycophants, I suspect he wondered whether his talents could have been applied in a more important direction.

His economy of words was amusingly described to me by a New York socialite and beauty, Caroline Cushing. She had spent a week staying with Mark in his Pelham Crescent house, during which time the only words he addressed to here were 'You are standing in front of the set.'

Another aspect of Mark's character was that he never spoke of his distinguished father, the artist Sir Oswald Birley. I would judge both Mark and Robin as kind-hearted individuals whose quest for the best occasionally required steely leadership. It is a remarkable dynasty, not excluding India Jane, an artist of consequence, and Mark's ex-wife, Annabel, a handsome lady of character and a devoted mother.

A Stately Liability in Kent

THE FIRST VISCOUNT De L'Isle and Dudley (known as Bill) is the only individual to have earned the right to display three quite different but wholly admirable suffixes to his name – Holder of the Victoria Cross, A Knight of the Garter and a Fellow of the Institute of Chartered Accountants. As it happens, I am a close friend of his son, Philip, and daughter-in-law, Isobel.

As a result, I have enjoyed many happy days shooting at Penshurst, their stately liability in Kent, and often found myself at breakfast or dinner facing the portrait of our hero by John Ward and pondering what sort of man he really was. The portrait, of him in his Garter Robes, is certainly that of an aristocrat and he wears a flinty, wintry look about those patrician features.

Not only did Bill hold the VC, KG and FCCA, but he was also a Privy Councillor, holder of the GCVO and the GCMG and had married the daughter of another holder of the Victoria Cross, Field Marshal Lord Gort. He had also been Governor-General of Australia and Secretary of State for Air. It was in the latter capacity that he visited Singapore and Malaya (still colonies) in 1952, prompting the editor of the *Straits Times* to instruct one of his journalists to cover Lord De L'Isle's visit and find out *who Dudley is*! It is actually a courtesy title conferred on an ancestor in 1835, for what reason I have been unable to discern.

During a brief interregnum between these lofty activities, he had an excursion into City life as Chairman of Phoenix Assurance, and it is surely much to his credit that he applied himself to earning the right to attach FCCA to that other string of letters. I assume that he was driven to earn some money, as winning the Victoria Cross, not to mention all the rest, carried no financial benefit. It was during this sojourn in the City of London that he revealed that he was not only a hero, but also a human being. At that time, I was labouring away between the hours of 10am and 3:30pm at the Ionian Bank (and Country Club as we gaily referred to it) and one of their clients was a celebrated entrepreneur, Pat Matthews, founder of First National Finance Corporation (FNFC), a well-known secondary banking/ property operation in the 1960s and 1970s. Pat (father-in-law of Sir Lloyd Dorfman, the philanthropist and founder of Travelex) was a clever, handsome and ingenious individual. He had founded FNFC in 1963.

All was going well until the secondary banking crash of 1973. FNFC eventually fell into the arms of the Bank of England, in the so-called 'lifeboat' operation for the various 'secondary' banks, including Keyser Ullman, London County and other smaller concerns. Matthews, although like most other entrepreneurs very much a loner, had had the wisdom and the skill to persuade De L'Isle to assume the FNFC Chairmanship. De L'Isle was not only physically and morally courageous, but he was extremely intelligent and, as David Kynaston states in *The City of London: Volume IV*, 'had been Governor-General of Australia but could also read a balance sheet'. De L'Isle had been introduced to Pat Matthews by Jocelyn Hambro, whose eponymous bank had formed a favourable view of him.

Lord De L'Isle and Pat Matthews made an interesting pair – the steely aristocrat and the clever and pugnacious entrepreneur. In some respects, the Secondary Banking Crisis and the establishment of the so-called 'lifeboat' by the Bank of England has a resemblance to the Guinness Affair, in the sense that events in the City moved so fast that new rules were required. The architects of the 'lifeboat' were Gordon Richardson, the Governor, and Sir Jasper Hollom. A handsome Bank of England lifer (who lived to nearly a hundred), Hollom was a reasonable, as well as a competent, man. The 'lifeboat' was by no means a unanimously supported scheme. Designed to arrest the ripple effect of the failure of the so-called secondary banks, it required the support of the clearing banks, who were by no means sure that it was in their interests to rescue their competitors, for that is what some of them had become. It is greatly to Hollom's credit that he persuaded some powerful iconoclasts to support his scheme.

De L'Isle and Matthews fought their corner, but, by 1976, Matthews was forced to abandon ship and he and his colleagues departed from the Board of FNFC. He did so with his dignity and reputation intact, almost alone of the secondary banking pioneers. For that, as he would have been the first to acknowledge, he owed a great personal debt to Lord De L'Isle who, having assumed the Chairmanship, never flinched during some challenging contests with Sir Jasper. De L'Isle died in 1991.

Noblesse Oblige: Princess Margaret, the Butler and the Peas

Princess Margaret conceived a great passion for a pleasant young man, Roddy Llewellyn. He was not known to me, so I was surprised to receive a call from a courtier asking if we could meet to discuss a very sensitive matter. This transpired to be a request as to whether I would consider providing employment to Llewellyn ... and should I do so it would not go unrecognised. I agreed to see Llewellyn and, since he was unqualified in the realms of geology or geophysics, I could not see my way to offering him employment. However, I did offer to take him on as an intern for two months so we could determine whether he had any useful qualities, however improbable this would be.

After a couple of weeks he suddenly disappeared. By this time, I was aware that he was Princess Margaret's inamorato. I thought no more about it, although there had begun to be references in the press to his disappearance.

One evening shortly afterwards I got another Llewellyn-focused call, this time from a friend of the Princess. 'Could you come and have dinner tomorrow evening at our house, as Princess Margaret particularly wants to talk to you.' I naturally said I would, although I felt a mild sense of foreboding.

When I turned up at the host's bijou house in Chelsea, it emerged that the lady of the house was ill in bed with the flu, so we sat down to dinner *à trois*. Our host had generously hired an elderly butler from an agency for the evening, but he was clearly somewhat nervous at his first royal assignment – at least his hands were shaking, so I generously assumed it was case of nerves rather than a case of whisky.

In any event dinner progressed, throughout which the Princess smoked incessantly. It was immediately apparent that she was in a terrible state of anxiety about the disappearance of her boyfriend and was hoping that I, perhaps the last person to have seen him, might have some clue as to why he had gone, not to mention *where* he had gone. Since I could not answer either question the evening was unfolding unsteadily, and throughout the proceedings the Princess was offensive to our hapless butler, whom she practically reduced to tears. Inevitably he was shaking so much that he upset a dish of peas all over the table, and she let rip at him.

At this point my host left the dining room, either to minister to his sick wife upstairs or to find a replacement for the peas in the kitchen. By now I had become somewhat nauseated by her Llewellyn obsession and protective of the ancient butler, so I let rip myself and told her what I thought of her bullying manner. She evinced no remorse and shortly after departed the house and my life.

A Singular Woman

URING OUR LIVES some of us are fortunate enough to encounter another
human being who stands apart and
who makes an immediate and lasting impres-
sion. Such was the case of me and two women,
one of whom I married. The other I vividly
recall meeting at a dinner party at the then
house of Demetri Marchessini on the corner
of Walton Street and Beauchamp Place. It was
1969. Across the round table sat the most beautiful girl I had ever seen, with raven-black hair
and perfect white teeth. She was Annabel 'Tessa'

Fraser, then married to Lord Reay, although separated at this point. I was twenty-nine, spoilt, just out of the Army and embarking on a meteoric two years at the beginning of the North Sea oil boom. The following two weeks were heady to say the least. One key moment was lunch at a restaurant on the corner of the King's Road and Alexander Square, where we resolved to elope.

Tessa, however, had many other suitors and protectors who somehow intervened, resulting in a torrid forty-eight hours without the ultimate romantic act eventuating. Amongst her lengthy list of admirers were Tony Lambton and Richard Soames, neither of whom gave me any cause for encouragement. Nonetheless, we had a highly charged relationship, including a week on a boat in Greece and days at Ophemert Castle, the Reay family property near Tiel in Holland.

She remained married to Hugh Reay during this giddy time (for me). Reay was experiencing a challenging period in his life which rendered him aloof and silent (almost Trappist), leading me to bestow on him the sobriquet 'chatty'! I recall seeing Hugh one day sitting at his desk in his enormous house in Wilton Crescent. He was staring at a blank piece of paper.

'What are you doing Hugh?' I enquired.

'I am working on my approach' came the enigmatic response.

All this derived from Hugh's experience with a certain Dutch psychiatrist, whom he had been seeing over some years. The psychiatrist had first appeared when Tessa, after her marriage, had developed anxiety about her first pregnancy. While alleviating Tessa's concerns the man cast a spell over Hugh and virtually ruled his life for five years, during which time Hugh would scarcely cross the road without consulting his controller in Holland. Hugh and Tessa had three children: Aeneas, Ned and Laura. Aeneas, named after his grandfather, is a distinguished businessman and working member of the House of Lords, as was his father who despite the five-year control was a most intelligent and courteous individual. Ned is my godson and also runs a successful business as well as the sporting estates for his stepfather, Henry Keswick. Ned has recently married Emily, a clever and beautiful lawyer with a Hong Kong family background. Laura lives quietly in Devon.

In 1985 Tessa married Henry Keswick, Hong Kong plutocrat and grandee, a marriage which happily endured the rest of her life. Tessa was gradually drawn to politics after her marriage and with her natural intelligence allied to a competitive streak she evolved rapidly into a formidable operator. Initially she stood as a Tory candidate for Inverness before working indefatigably for Kenneth Clarke whilst he was Home Secretary. She then took over the role of Director of the Centre for Policy Studies, from where she radiated ideas and energy. Henry provided the stability that enabled Tessa to conduct her political life both from the Centre for Policy Studies in Tufton Street and via her salon in their house around the corner in Smith Square. Tessa was cast in a heroic mould, her father being the legendary Second World War hero the 15th Lord Lovat. She took after him in many ways – but above all in being aristocratic but never condescending. She was tough but never mean and was always fun and skilfully iconoclastic in conversation.

Tessa Keswick died in September 2022. She gave so much more than she ever took from life.

Nautical Authors

Georce Millar and Lord Stanley of Alderley are two quite different individuals united by their love of the sea and their authorship of classic yachting memoirs. As the honorary librarian of Britain's premier yacht club, I get to have more than my fair share of access to long-since-forgotten maritime books. The library itself is a haven for the yachtsman, with editions dealing with every aspect of marine activity, with one proviso: they should not only be rare but more importantly be readable. Accordingly, whether the member be concerned with rules, etiquette, design or with the history of yachting and of yacht clubs or aspects of Naval history, he will find whatever he requires on the welcoming shelves of the beautiful library, which is such a pleasure simply to visit.

Yachtsmen (or no doubt yachters as they will need to be called consonant with the prevailing tyranny!) tend thankfully to write up their experiences for the benefit of the rest of us and I have, as part of my duties, read many works which may otherwise not have come my way.

In fact, I had the honour of knowing George Millar, the first of my two selected authors, having written him a fan letter as a result of reading *A White Boat from England* (1951) and *Oyster River* (1963). As recorded by fellow war hero Sir Robin Hooper, Millar, unusually for a sailor, was colour-blind and had difficulty discerning the difference between red and green, which he disclosed to Hooper as they were navigating a boat through the busy shipping lanes of Le Havre! As it happened, we were both members of the same yacht club. George was born in 1910 and I in 1940, but we became close friends. He was lowland Scottish by birth, educated at Loretto from where he went to Cambridge and trained to be an architect. Serendipity revealed his gift for the English language and led him to spend five years in Paris with the *Daily Telegraph* and the *Daily Express*. He enlisted in the Rifle Brigade in 1939 and there began five years of constant and challenging soldiering, both as a combatant and subsequently, from 1944, as an SOE officer attached to the Maquis. His endeavours earned him the Distinguished Service Order, the Military Cross, the Croix de Guerre and the Légion d'honneur. Happily for posterity he produced virtually the first Second World War memoir, *Maquis,* in 1945, followed by *Horned Pigeon* in 1946. Both of these must rate in the first rank of Second World War memoirs.

George was a slightly built, fair-haired and undeniably handsome man, aged twenty-eight when the war began. He experienced the gamut of military life including capture and escape, which he chronicles vividly in these two volumes. After the war he not only became a highly successful military historian but decided to farm in Dorset near Cerne Abbas after marrying Isabel Hardwell in 1945 (a busy year for him). Thereafter he continued to write, including a history of the Bruneval Raid in 1974, but it was his sailing reminiscences which mark him out, and it rather perplexes me that he is not more celebrated. Perhaps because he was devoid of ego, but his heroism, his felicity with pen and his nautical competence render him a man of exceptional talent. He died in 2005, aged ninety-four.

My second and perhaps surprising choice of nautical author is Lord Stanley of Alderley. There hangs in White's Club a conversation piece painted in 1948 by Simon Elwes which depicts twenty-seven of the Club's prominent contemporary members, including Douglas Fairbanks, Lord Camrose, Randolph Churchill, the Duke of Devonshire and a dark-haired slightly built figure – Ed Stanley. Other than his gallant war service Ed Stanley could not have been more unlike George Millar, except that he also produced a delightful yachting memoir, *Sea Peace*, a beautifully written account of various voyages around the British Isles, mostly with his close friend Roger Chetwode, son of the Field Marshal, who died in 1940 and to whom Stanley wrote the following ode, which I believe warrants republishing:

We who so often sailed the sea
Each with the other, both together;
Easily running down the lee,
Or grappling our hard-won way to weather.
A pattern of life we formed, we two,
Sharing the pleasures and pain,
An intimate understanding crew,
Equally one in sunshine and rain.
Now you have put to sea alone
Where shall I find the easy laughter,
Begun with the sailing Aimée Leone
Down to Joanna in Denmark, and after.
The Sun is setting. Long sad days,
Each one by you unblest,
Stand bleak against its dying rays
Towards the darkening West.
The narrow seas we knew so well
Are tears too few to shed,
Each clanging bell-buoys rings its knell
For you, untimely dead.
The velvet black of night your pall,
The stars your diadem,
The moaning gales descant to all
Your mournful requiem.
Eheu fugaces! Oh my Prince,
I'm old, my day is gone,
And Spring has turned to Winter since
You sailed into the Sun.
But as I wait the day when I
My earthly cables sever,
I shall recoil the jovial high
Adventurous bold endeavour;
And grateful happiness shall lie
Within my heart for ever.

When the war began Stanley joined the RNVR, reaching the rank of Lieutenant Commander. He inherited a large fortune which was greatly diminished by two sets of death duties, by his zest for life and for women, including five marriages – a record even for a member of White's. A friend of Evelyn Waugh, Cyril Connolly and Peter Quennell, he features frequently in Waugh's diaries and letters. Hilaire Belloc was a close friend of Stanley's father, Arthur. Stanley married amongst others Mrs Douglas Fairbanks (who eventually became Mrs Clark Gable). Although something of a hell-raiser he was an interesting man and, despite his wives, or because of them, something of a loner, which partially accounts for his love of the sea. He was intellectual and indeed was on the short-list to write a biography of Belloc.

He wrote *Sea Peace* in 1955, which contains charming accounts of voyages in a succession of yachts between 1932 and 1946, interrupted by his war service in the RNVR. Stanley got into some trouble as a result of this book for lampooning his friend Peter Rodd, or Prod as he was known, Nancy Mitford's husband. Stanley, however, had a real capacity for friendship, as is revealed by the touching poetic tribute. He died in 1971.

.

The Guinness Affair

ONE OF THE causes célèbres of the 1980s was the so-called Guinness Affair. Two companies, Guinness and Argyll Foods, were competing to acquire the Distillers Company, and trouble ensued after the revelation by an American arbitrageur, Ivan Boesky, that he had been rewarded for participating in a plan to support the Guinness share price. An enquiry was launched into the circumstances surrounding this support process. The first curious feature of this was that the investigation focused solely on the activities of the Guinness camp, whereas the Argyll camp were conducting an identical campaign but were not prosecuted.

It was also the case that the government of the day, led by Margaret Thatcher, was highly sensitive to any suggestion that it had a tendency to be soft on white-collar crime, and a general election was imminent. In those days the value of a company was determined simply by its share market value, and hence the share prices of the combatants was all-important. If a company intended to engage in a support operation of its own share price it was required by law to obtain the agreement of its shareholders. This had not been done. The advisers to the Guinness camp were Morgan Grenfell, of which the principal executive was the clever and articulate Roger Seelig. Their brokers were Cazenove. After consultation with Michael Howard, who was a junior minister in the Department of Trade and Industry, it was decided to prosecute – firstly those actively involved in the support operation (and beneficiaries of substantial fees), known as Guinness One, and then to prosecute the advisers, in particular Seelig and David Mayhew of Cazenove, urbane and competent (Guinness Two). In the event Morgan Grenfell elected not to stand behind Roger Seelig, whereas the

Cazenove partnership did support Mayhew. But Guinness Two never eventuated due to Seelig's ill health.

It so happened that all the defendants in Guinness One, that is those who participated in the share support scheme, were Jewish and their eventual conviction and imprisonment led to suggestions that they were victims of an anti-Jewish conspiracy. I find that is not the case at all. The Prime Minister was a most ardent admirer of the Jewish race, the politician who gave the prosecution the green light, the able and decent Michael Howard, is Jewish, and Sir Denis Henry, the judge, was also Jewish. The latter had had little experience of this sector of the law and was perhaps a surprising choice to sit in the case, although he was undoubtedly able. It was necessary for a judge of intellectual strength to maintain control of the complexities of the case, which lasted for months. Where the defendants were unlucky was not that they were Jewish, but that the Jewish judge was a high-minded left-leaning individual who had little tolerance of rich men becoming richer without expending any effort (his Chambers had incidentally spawned two Labour Lord Chancellors). It is certainly easy to sympathise with the Guinness One defendants as a result of their harsh treatment, particularly as none of the advisors had their day in Court. And as I have said, additionally the Argyll camp were not prosecuted at all. No one knows why not.

Guinness occurred at a time of hectic activity in the City, when the capitalisation of companies was reaching new levels. A new generation of iconoclastic businessmen were riding high and were operating within grey areas, with the merchant banks being expected by their clients to devise new and original methods of enabling them to prosper by acquisition, whilst ensuring that they kept their clients within 'The Rules'. But what were those rules and how to do you control strong wills, and brash and arrogant figures such as Boesky, Ephraim Margulies, Meshulam Riklis of Schenley Industries (Distillers' American distributor) – all participants in the Guinness share support picture. The Morgan Grenfell indemnification scheme with Guinness was not illegal, but the scale of it caused anxiety at the Bank of England.

After a period of introspection and criticism, the prosecution of the Guinness support 'committee' was set in motion. In my view, the 'support committee' should not have been prosecuted and certainly not imprisoned. Christopher Reeves, the widely liked and admired Chief Executive of Morgan Grenfell (who gallantly fell on his sword eventually, unlike his Chairman, Lord Catto) is quoted in Kynaston's *Volume IV* of his *History of the City of London* as saying to the *Financial Times* in reflection on Guinness, 'Some say we got round the rules, I think we innovated. Clients want to deal with people with original ideas. So new rules have to be created. We must not believe that rules are written in tablets of stone.'

From this distance, it appears to me that those prosecuted in the Guinness Affair were victims of confusion in a grey legal area, of a high-minded (but competent) judge and of political uncertainty about how to control white-collar excess (or 'crime', depending on your politics). It would be not unreasonable for them to be pardoned.

A City Institution

THE STOCKBROKING FIRM of Strauss, Turnbull was founded in 1938 by Robert and Ronald Strauss, and New Zealand shipping heir Jim Turnbull, as a breakaway company from Vickers, da Costa. Under the direction of Ronald's son, Derek, it evolved after the war into a creative and courageous firm which acted in many celebrated City sagas including the Guinness Affair and various corporate battles involving 'Tiny' Rowland's Lonrho group. Ronald's cousin, Julius, a refugee from Germany, joined later and single-handedly virtually invented the Eurobond market.

Derek, now eighty-three, served in the Royal Navy and maintained a boat throughout most of his life. He married Nicky, the daughter of Diana, granddaughter of Sir John Lavery and half-sister of Lady (Ann) Sempill. Nicky brought with her a dowry of oil paintings by Lavery which must rank as the largest collection of his work in private hands.

During the last war Ann Sempill joined the WRNS (Women's Royal Naval Service) and by a curious chance was stationed in my house on the White Cliffs of Dover where she was charged with the task of listening in to the wireless traffic of enemy shipping navigating the Straits of Dover. I once asked her whether she found it a satisfying task. It was wonderful, she sighed, doubtless referring to the Royal Artillery officers also stationed there!

After the war she married a Lieutenant Colonel Stuart Chant, who had been decorated for gallantry during the commando raid on Saint-Nazaire. By another curious chance I have an oil painting of him by Lavery in the uniform of the Black Watch.

Strauss, Turnbull, an imaginative firm, conducted much arbitrage with the Cape (in practice Johannesburg) and developed a tendency to support the mining sector. This has been followed by Derek and Nicky's two able sons Jamie and Toby. In the 1970s an Australian geologist, Fred Collander, became associated with Strauss, Turnbull. He had partnered Sir Val Duncan in the formation of Rio Tinto-Zinc and scored a number of mining successes including ownership of a nickel prospect at Francistown in Botswana. Fred suggested to Derek that the firm should advance the Francistown seed capital, which Derek had been gallantly funding himself. In the event the robust Swedish oil tycoon Adolf Lundin took over. With tragic irony Fred died from metal poisoning contracted whilst down a mine in South Africa.

There then arrived on the scene the London-based Greek brothers Demetri and Alexander Marchessini, known irreverently by the *Spectator* columnist Taki as 'Arsenic and Old Lace'. They were the progeny of a shipowner who had skilfully exited the shipping business during one of its sporadic highs. He died and the boys inherited a large fortune of which they enjoyed the fruits whilst not conspicuously replenishing its depleting size. Whilst both were undeniably intelligent, Alexander the laid-back younger brother tended to defer to Demetri, a man of definite (and latterly eccentric) opinions. He was a good friend of mine, but he became controversial, to say the least, scorning any criticism of his reactionary views.

They were both handsome and cut quite a swathe through female London. They both enjoyed and sought out riskier investments and when chance introduced them to Fred Collander they invested in Francistown Nickel. It was not long before Fred found Demetri's forcibly expressed opinions unacceptable, and he realised that Demetri lacked an understanding of mining in general and of Francistown in particular. This paved the way for Patrick Quirk, a robust Rhodesian, who certainly did understand mining, to buy out the Marchessini interest.

Quirk had mining in his blood, and he had courage and confidence and quickly realised that Francistown had enormous potential. And indeed it rapidly evolved into a huge concern, making large fortunes for Collander, for Patrick Quirk and his colleagues and a smaller fortune for the admirable and honourable Kim Fraser, one of Lord Lovat's four sons, all alas now deceased.

Kim was a Strauss, Turnbull partner and

became the Chairman of Francistown. Derek continued to hire a galaxy of City talent including Paul Irby, diligent and discreet, and Lord Roger Manners, enthusiastic, inquisitive and loyal. Derek went on to direct an enterprise which succeeded in being unorthodox and yet highly respected. One of the City's best. After Big Bang and the arrival of the American banks, the under-capitalised and overtaxed British brokerage community gratefully submitted to Wall Street's embrace. Derek had skilfully pre-empted Big Bang by three years through a joint venture with Société Générale, a harmonious arrangement.

THE STAY-AT-HOME EXECUTIVE

A S THE REGULATORS closed in on business disclosure, with the introduction of benefits in kind and the requirement for companies' reports and accounts to reveal salaries, options and in some cases the number of Board meetings attended by directors, there remained one glaring (or welcome) lacuna – business flights. Although they belong to the business itself, the 'points' earned attach to the employee and so do not attract tax. I often thought so much of business travel was totally unnecessary, and that there should be another column in reports and accounts revealing the travel costs (including class) of the executives. I have always considered Sir Alfred Chester Beatty to have exemplified the value of the stay-at-home executive. He built up the largest copper mining company in the world – Selection Trust. He was responsible for the discovery of what became known as the copper belt in Central Africa, and never once travelled further from home in Kensington Palace Gardens than to the City of London (admittedly in the back of a huge Rolls-Royce).

He lived in style in what is now the Russian Embassy and amassed not only a huge fortune but also, mostly housed in Kensington Park Gardens, a unique collection of Persian manuscripts, together with an important collection of French Impressionists. It was his intention that the people of the United Kingdom, his adopted home, should be the beneficiary of these two collections. Labyrinthine negotiations occurred with HM Treasury, seeking various tax and death duty exemptions, but the tax man refused to cooperate. President De Valera was alerted to this impasse, and being advised that the collection was the finest of manuscripts and decorative arts from the Islamic world, India, China, Japan and Turkey in private hands, he summoned Chester Beatty to Dublin and assured him that, should he donate his cornucopia to the Irish people, not only would he pay no tax, but he would be given honorary Irish citizenship together with a State Funeral. As indeed was the case. The President was as good as his word, and Chester Beatty's mortal remains were hauled through the streets of Dublin before the bemused gaze of the populace, who were wondering whether this funeral was of a hitherto unknown IRA hero!

Such intransigence has led to the loss to Britain of at least two other collections destined for national museums and galleries – the Thyssen Collection of paintings now in Madrid, and the Calouste Gulbenkian Collection, now in Lisbon.

It was sad that Chester Beatty turned his back on his adoptive home (he was originally American) for whom he had earned so much wealth. Churchill conceded this by awarding him a belated knighthood in 1954. This was not only in recognition of the riches he had secured for Great Britain, but also for his work during the Second World War. Chester Beatty had a very useful war and it is frankly incredible that it was not until nearly ten years after the war that he was knighted. He performed invaluable services on two levels. Firstly, his knowledge of strategic minerals was unrivalled and as a result he was co-opted as Vice Chairman of the so-called UK Commercial Commission by Oliver Lyttelton, President of the Board of Trade. The UK CC was in effect charged with the task of denying the enemy materials and minerals of strategic importance by purchase. This Board, led by Lord Swinton, included other than Chester Beatty, Sir Leonard Payton, Jack Hambro and Brigadier John Shearer, a director of military intelligence. Secondly, Chester Beatty applied his inventive brain in support of Churchill's famous instruction to the special forces to 'set Europe ablaze'.

He had a son, Chet, who could give the Ancient Mariner a run for his money, although he donated large sums to medical charities. His company, Selection Trust, was purchased by BP in an unfortunate move into copper and is no more. It joins a long and melancholy list of vanished British companies such as ICI, BTR, GEC and many others.

Gold Mining in Africa

IN 1995 I was blessed with the benefit both of 100,000 ounces of gold production a year from two mines in Zimbabwe and one in Ghana, as well as a talented team including Michael Martineau from BP Minerals and Peter Cowley. The latter became not only an invaluable and trusted colleague but also an enduring friend and we have recently teamed up in business again for the third time. At that time, I had decided that we should look beyond Ghana and Zimbabwe, and Tanzania was selected to be our next objective. This was more successful than we had ever expected. For as long as it lasted it was an interesting lesson in national integrity on Tanzania's side and technical enterprise on our part. Peter Cowley, Cluff Resources Technical Director, made a number of visits to Tanzania, and in particular to an area on the shores of Lake Victoria, Geita, where there had been intermittent production from the 1940s until it ceased in 1967 with the onset of President Nyerere's doctrinaire socialism. A well-disposed Tanzanian-based shareholder in the company, Craig Niven, introduced us to a most charming retired civil servant, Freddie Machauru, who had at one stage been the Minister of Posts and Telecommunications, and who became our local representative.

Eager as we were to start exploration, it emerged that an Egyptian company owned key Geita ground but, as they had been supine in fulfilling their commitments, the Tanzanian government sought international arbitration to cancel their rights which was successful and, three years later, in 1994, we were awarded the Geita licence. By this time the geological appeal of Tanzania together with its government's investor-friendly approach had resulted in a deluge of companies seeking mining rights. Happily, the Finance Ministry led by Colonel

Jakaya Kikwete were steadfast in their support for us.

Anglo-American and others by now were professing their incredulity that a junior company had secured such promising ground, and I gave much thought to how we could further extend our holding in the face of such animosity. The turning point occurred at a dinner at the Cavalry and Guards Club in London attended by Sir Thomas Pilkington, our shrewd Deputy Chairman, Peter Cowley, Freddie Machauru, and the imposing Permanent Secretary at the Mining Ministry. This occurred in a pleasant room known as the Bridle Room in memory of an illustrious previous member, Major General Jack d'Avigdor-Goldsmid. The minister impressed us all by appearing immaculately dressed in a white tuxedo and conversation, initially of a military bias, flourished. I then delivered my trump card which was an offer – should Geita evolve into a commercial mine – to return 20 per cent of it to the government of Tanzania which, after refunding us pro-rata our costs to date, they could use as the basis of a new state mining company to be listed on the Dar es Salaam stock exchange, which would not only be highly profitable but would also enable the government to monitor the performance of other mining investors. Shortly afterwards we were additionally awarded the UN ground as well, thereby astounding the large, inert corporations. The reasons, however, were simple and legitimate – we had explored rapidly and thoroughly and had on our team trained Tanzanian geologists and geophysicists (some through the under-used but effective so-called Chevening Scholarships – endorsed in particular by Professor David Dilks, the enlightened Vice-Chancellor of the University of Hull at the time).

Geita fulfilled its promise, and it was manifestly obvious that it was to be one of Africa's largest gold mines. As a result, we were acquired (most reluctantly) by one of the rejected suitors, Ashanti Goldfields, and they were in turn acquired by Anglo-American. In 2005 Colonel Kikwete was elected President and served his country skilfully until 2015 when, alas, he was succeeded by a Covid-denying eccentric (who died of Covid). His successor, a Zanzibar lady, has already done much to build on the Kikwete legacy. Curiously Peter and I, together with other friends, are re-entering the Tanzania mining scene after an absence of twenty-three years.

My offer to return 20 per cent of the Geita

mine to the Tanzanian government, like a ticking bomb, must remain somewhere in a dusty cupboard in the Ministry of Mines.

Will 'English Sparkling Wine' ever rival Champagne? I now have a dog in this fight.

Princess Margaret – I fell from her grace after a sticky dinner.

L: Portrait of Lord De L'Isle in dress uniform.

R: Lord Methuen, who commanded the British troops at the Battle of Belmont.

The Battle of Belmont in the 2nd Boer War, 1899 – forgotten by many, but not by the Grenadiers.

Above: AC and Sir Edward Barry on Queen's Guard, 1960.

R: Emergence of the Guards Squadron SAS from the Borneo jungle, 1964. AC on the left.

R: Philip 'Chrome Dome' Haslett and Tom Richardson off the West African Coast, 1963.

Opposite: Guards dinner.

Boodle's on St James's – the card room there was surely the inspiration for the classic bridge scene in Ian Fleming's *Moonraker*.

The starter's hut at Royal St George's, the model for the golf club in Fleming's *Goldfinger*. The club could find no place for a picture of its most celebrated member.

The famous Billy Edgson – the 'Peter Pan of Mayfair'.

The open-pit at Geita – a gold mining coup and huge asset for Tanzania.

Prudhoe Bay oil fields in the 1970s – the largest in North America.

Below: A graveyard for oil rigs in Inverness. Now Britain ships in gas from the Middle East and USA at huge environmental cost.

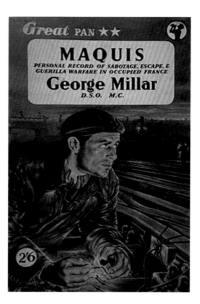

One of the very first Second World War memoirs, and in the first rank.

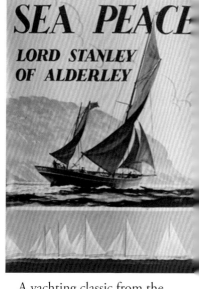

A yachting classic from the much-married Lord Stanley.

George Millar sailed his yacht *Serica* to the Riviera after the war, which gave rise to the classic but sadly neglected book *A White Boat from England*.

Conversation piece at White's, by Simon Elwes, including Douglas Fairbanks, Randolph Churchill, the Duke of Devonshire and Edward Stanley.

La Boisserie, family home of General de Gaulle at Colombey-les-Deux-Églises. We were duly impressed by the modesty and austerity of the great man's quarters.

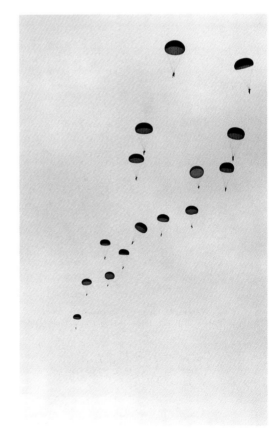

A stick of parachute jumpers – at least my comrades and I survived our drop into Macedonia during an incompetent NATO exercise in 1963. The same could not be said of our designated vehicle.

Clement Attlee – most
effective at dealing with bores.

Ashe Windham with a flyer
for my first book, *Get On
With It*, at the Castle of May.

Tessa Keswick – she stood apart.

Bribery

O N ONLY ONE occasion during fifty years of active business in Africa was it made clear to me that, unless I were to pay a bribe, our interests would be prejudiced or forfeited. It was over a possible gold mine in Sierra Leone, and the man demanding a bribe was an Englishman, not an African!

At the time (2005) the company which I then chaired owned a portfolio of gold interests in West Africa, including two gold mines in the Ivory Coast and Burkina Faso. We had also negotiated the acquisition of a gold discovery in Sierra Leone from Ronald Winston, an old friend of mine who had inherited it from his legendary father Harry Winston, the proprietor of the eponymous diamond company. This licence had originally been identified by a Professor of Geology at Columbia University. Harry acquired the licence and drilled a number of adits into a small range of hills, but interest faded during Sierra Leone's civil war.

Ronald and I often discussed how to revive this prospect and a prolonged and agreeable negotiation took place, mostly in his private office at the Harry Winston building on Fifth Avenue in New York, a room redolent of the triumphs and of the clients of the Winston family business, represented by a number of photographs and portraits. Ronald and I eventually agreed an arrangement whereby we issued shares in Cluff Resources in exchange for the licence. This all required the approval of the Ministry of Mines, then headed sequentially by two thoroughly experienced and decent ministers. Although bringing the gold mines into production in Burkina Faso and the Ivory Coast made the primary demands on our resources, both executive and financial, we got to work with a team led by an experienced Zimbabwean geologist, Douglas Chikohora, and subsequently by Peter Spivey, a charming New Zealander who had made his home in Senegal. In London, the affairs of the company were largely concentrated in the hands of the Finance Director Peter Gardiner, and the Company Secretary, Catherine Apthorpe – both agreeable and intelligent colleagues.

There was some disagreement technically at what was the appropriate way ahead: should it be addressed as having the potential to be a major producer, with a 200,000 ounce per annum production (the Spivey plan), or should a more cautious and modular approach be taken, with an initial 50,000 ounce open pit mine being favoured (which I recall was my own, Ronald Winston's and Douglas Chikohora's favoured route). At any rate, much time and money were spent to determine the way forward and establish a base camp deep in the jungle – an eight-hour drive from Freetown.

Whilst all this was going on a new minister was appointed, an arrogant man who claimed to have contacts with the country's President (although he never produced any evidence of that). I took an immediate dislike to him and developed a sense of foreboding. One day we were advised that his excellency was visiting London (where he apparently maintained a house) and that he wished to meet our executive team at the Sierra Leone High Commission to hear a progress report. This was agreed and I proposed that, since the meeting was at 11am, we could invite him and any of his Sierra Leone officials to lunch afterwards. Our team I recall consisted of Douglas Chikohora, Catherine Apthorpe and myself. When we were ushered into the High Commission meeting room I was surprised to see that, other than the minister, the only other individual present was an Englishman: slight, bald, paunchy and exuding self-importance. He was introduced to us as being 'David Massie, my Special Advisor'. No officials at all. I was taken aback by this – we were a public company, about to reveal price sensitive information to a high-ranking minister, and there at the meeting was an English private citizen of whom we had never heard. The meeting, however, proceeded, and we gave them our interpretation of the status of the project and the need for us to raise further capital to fund a drilling campaign.

After the meeting concluded we ushered the minister towards the taxi, which we had ordered to take us to lunch. At this point Massie made to get into the vehicle and I said to him 'I don't know who you are, and you are not invited to this lunch.' Nonetheless he was by this time in the taxi, and I resigned myself to accepting this fait accompli whilst being carefully on my guard.

Shortly after this he requested a meeting at our office, as he needed to convey a message to us from the minister, which he described as being urgent and highly price sensitive. With great misgivings I agreed to this. There was now no doubt in my mind that this man was an obnoxious bully with no standing other than a questionable relationship with the minister. Equally, he was highly intelligent and dangerous. At the meeting he said he was really acting in our interests as we should be aware that the minister considered that our progress at the mine was not acceptable and that to avoid a conflict with the Ministry we should pay Massie a retainer to enable him to 'protect our interests'. This – after consulting with Peter Gardiner and Catherine Apthorpe – we declined to do.

It was not long before the denouement unfolded. I received a summons from Massie to meet him and the minister at Massie's office in New Bond Street. He introduced himself as the Chairman and CEO of an investment company, this being their office. I had no alternative but to attend this meeting, although it is of course highly irregular for such a minister to conduct such a meeting to 'review our licence' with no other officials present and not on ministerial territory. I took Catherine Apthorpe with me. We were shown into a meeting room where there sat side by side the minister, Massie and no one else. I was invited to explain why more investment had not been forthcoming and warned that the minister was reviewing the status of our licences and was contemplating cancelling it for non-performance. We were then ushered from their presence, and Massie came down in the lift with us. His parting words were 'Make no mistake, the minister is deadly serious and is about to cancel your licence.'

Catherine and I were aghast at this, and of course at the forefront of our minds was where our duty lay with regard to the shareholders. Was this a threat with the objective of us signing up to some agreement to pay Massie (and, of course, the minister) some form of emolument. We agreed to take no action that evening. The minister had said that the next day he was flying to Washington on ministerial business and was accordingly unlikely to be back in Freetown until the following week. As it happened, the next day there was delivered to me by hand a letter from Massie. What the missive said was that the minister was deadly serious and that he intended to terminate the licence. However, it went on, were we to pay $10 million (in two instalments) to his business, he, Massie, would be entirely confident that, working in concert with us, he could retrieve the situation and persuade the minister to remove the threat to our title.

However, the Almighty intervened and Massie suffered a fatal stroke, thereby removing perhaps the most objectionable specimen I had met in fifty years of business experience. The minister was transferred and not heard from again.

Up and Down in Singapore

T HIS PHOTOGRAPH WAS taken on 7th November 1964 in the dining room of the Goodwood Park Hotel (prior to World War One it had been the German Embassy). It depicts a dinner to mark the emergence of the Guards Squadron SAS from the Borneo jungle the night before we returned to the UK. The Irish Guards were stationed in Singapore at Nee Soon Barracks at the time and two of their officers feature – John Lockwood on the left and John Morrogh-Bernard on the right, together with their wives. The blonde lady between Patrick Beresford and a rather emaciated Cluff is unknown. Tragedy attended the two Irish Guards: Morrogh-Bernard was shortly afterwards swept away to his death by an avalanche whilst skiing in Switzerland and one of the Lockwood children, Michael (my godson), died aged nineteen whilst on a trek through the highlands of Thailand. He was on a course with Jardines in Hong Kong where for long weekends it had become popular for the young to combine treks with other kinds of rest and recuperation, in particular the smoking of marijuana. Michael had asthma and the combination of the asthma, the marijuana and the altitude killed the poor boy.

John Lockwood left his wife, Hilly Warlow-Harry, shortly afterwards and married an Austrian Countess. All the men in the photograph bar myself are now dead.

Shortly before the dinner I had had an alarming experience whilst doing my final military parachute jump somewhere across the Causeway in Johore Bahru. When conducting a military jump it is the practice to bundle as many men as possible out of the plane as quickly as possible, so the jumps occur at about 800 feet above the ground. The parachutists are arranged in so-called 'sticks' of eight men, led by an officer, in this case myself. When the despatcher gave the order to jump I duly launched myself into space, at which point I realised that, whereas my stick was already on the ground, I remained suspended in the atmosphere and experienced the alarming sensation of going up not down! I had in fact been caught in some freak air pocket and after a long few seconds began my descent to join my colleagues. The photograph reveals me as looking rather skeletal after some months' immersion in the jungle, in contrast to Beresford who was glowing with health, having spent his time not in the jungle but in the Chinese coastal town of Sibu.

The Battle of Belmont

In November 2022 there was held a dinner in the Officers' Mess at St James's Palace, which is used by those officers who make up the King's Guard. The date was 23rd November, and the occasion was to mark the anniversary of the Battle of Belmont in 1899 between the Boers and a force under the command of Lord Methuen, which included the 3rd Battalion of the Grenadier Guards. Methuen was on his way to raise the siege of Kimberley when he was assaulted by two thousand Boer commandos at the Belmont kopje. Fierce fighting culminated in a bayonet charge which secured a British victory.

The guests were all officers who had served in the 3rd Battalion (which was disbanded in 1960) and were all accordingly of a certain age (that is, over eighty). Notwithstanding this challenging age qualification, as many as twenty Grenadiers were eligible, of whom eight attended, complemented by Evelyn Webb-Carter, a previous Major General commanding London District; James Gatehouse, the Grenadier Regimental Adjutant; and the three officers on guard that day led by Major Hugo Cartwright, whose father was one of the veterans attending, together with two other serving officers (who were due to fly to Iraq the following day). As my wife drove me to the entrance to the Officers' Mess within St James's Palace there was a small group of elderly but soldierly men picked out in the car's headlights. 'That looks like your comrades-in-arms,' she said, as indeed they were.

We advanced into Pump Court and began the ascent of the steps that lead into the Officers' Mess, and which seemed considerably steeper than when I last climbed them as a twenty-year-old officer in 1960. Otherwise, it was gratifying to note that virtually nothing has changed in that dining room since then, other than the absence of the legendary Mess Sergeant, Tom Yardley, who presided over the Officers' Mess for over fifty years. In particular the oil portraits of Queen Victoria and Lord Kitchener remain as they were, although a rather louche screen of Edwardian high jinks has been moved out of sight. Already on parade and in very good trim were John Smiley (one time adjutant of the 3rd Battalion), Tom Cook (Norfolk grandee), David Gordon Lennox, a retired Major General, Nicholas Hunloke, retired stockbroker, and Nigel Cartwright.

The dinner had last been held on 23rd November 1949 at the Dorchester Hotel on the fiftieth anniversary of the battle. It is admirable that the regiment does not forget, as the battle cost the lives of thirty-six Grenadiers with one hundred and fourteen being wounded in the successful bayonet assault. The evening was a happy if nostalgic one, at least for me – I joined the 3rd Battalion in November 1959 and the Senior Subaltern detailed to show me around Wellington Barracks was none other than Christopher Fagan, then, as now, courteous and firm, every inch the Guardsman and hardly changed at all despite the sixty-three-year interval. Meanwhile, The Remembrance Trust charity is poised to restore those graves in far-off South Africa.

THE RACE TO THRACE

D URING THE COLD War one of the
weak spots in NATO's defence was
judged to be the Macedonian Gap in
Northern Greece. There were many other such
weak spots, but NATO command ordained in
1963 that in order to deter the Soviet military
from identifying Macedonia as a suitable place
in which to launch the Third World War,
NATO would draw the Soviets' attention to it
by holding the first joint NATO and Turkish
aerial exercises, parachuting twenty thousand
troops together with their vehicles on to

the Macedonian plain. My battalion of the Grenadier Guards was involved in this exciting scheme, which had two striking shortcomings. The first was a failure of planning: it did not occur to anyone to advise the inhabitants of Macedonia that they were about to be invaded by twenty thousand men and vehicles and, being mostly rural peasantry, their military identification skills were not so developed that they would discern the difference between friendly parachutists – be they French, British, Italian, Turkish – or the hostile Soviet variety. The population therefore jumped to the conclusion that this was the much-heralded Soviet invasion of Europe, loaded their belongings onto horse-drawn carts and headed south en masse. The directors of this exercise consequently spent much of the following two weeks not in testing their defensive skills so much as rounding up and reassuring the panicking peasantry.

The second issue was more pertinent to me personally, tiny cog in the NATO wheel that I was. Major Tom Richardson, my wry, clever, iconoclastic and very lazy Company Commander, together with a Rifle Brigade officer whose name I recall was Sam Shephard and others, were deputed as 'Marshals' to be on the Dropping Zone (DZ) when the troops and transport were scheduled to descend from the sky. One of these vehicles was a brand-new Land Rover dedicated to Major Tom and me, into which we were to leap and hare away from the DZ whilst effecting some order into the movement of hundreds of other vehicles and thousands of parachutists. Major Tom and I had some foreboding about our competence to discharge this responsibility. However, this was not put to the test. As the vehicles – three-ton trucks and armoured carriers of various types – cascaded to the ground, we observed that one of the Land Rovers was plummeting to earth as one of its parachutes had failed to open, and when it hit the ground it resembled more an empty sardine tin than a brand-new Land Rover.

'You know something, Algy…' Major Tom observed laconically, 'I have a nasty feeling that that erstwhile Land Rover will turn out to have our name on it.'

'Surely not,' I retorted, but as a sea of keen soldiery identified their vehicles and speedily vacated the DZ it became evident that the ex-Land-Rover was indeed ours. Naturally no provision for this eventuality had occurred to those same controlling staff who had previously failed to warn the locals of our arrival. The

Brigade Major I shall not forget, on account of his name as much as anything else. He was Major Sir Gregor Macgregor of Macgregor, Baronet of the Scots Guards, born with a sense of humour and charm deficiency. He indicated that it was somehow the fault of Major Tom and me that the Land Rover parachute had failed to open. As we stood haplessly on the margin of the DZ, he snarled: 'Make your own way to Thrace!' – not an injunction I had ever thought would confront me. The flip side of this inconvenience rapidly occurred to Major Tom and me: namely that we were probably well out of this mad escapade and could look forward to a Brigade-Major-free few days whilst we made alternative arrangements. These took the form of two elderly horses. As a form of locomotion, the horse is my least favourite, but nonetheless the Major and I enjoyed three days in leisurely pursuit of our comrades, during which we familiarised ourselves with the countryside and its wine, spending the nights in our sleeping bags in a haze of ouzo whilst composing ourselves to sleep to the surprisingly loud sound of copulating turtles.

I became very fond of the Major and, after our return to Kandahar Barracks at Tidworth, I used to accompany him on his frequent excursions to dinner at Overton's at the foot of St James's followed by unprofitable hours at Crockford's Club, then a casino in Carlton House Terrace. Poor, clever Tom Richardson then left the Army, and, other than completing *The Times* crossword puzzle, contributed very little to our world, being congenitally incapable of work.

OIL AND GAS

I N MARCH 2023 it was announced that John
Grundon OBE had died, at the age of ninety-
one. This melancholy event stirred no
interest from the press, but he was virtually the
last of the senior management at BP during the
heady days of North Sea oil and gas exploration
and development. That the North Sea was a
geological gift from above there had been no
doubt, but it was the technical challenge which
was so dramatic, as was the response of the oil
companies, predominantly American but also

approximately thirty per cent British.

Had Mrs Sturgeon been at the helm of the Scottish government it would probably not have happened at all. Happily, she was not, and the British government retained absolute control over licensing policy. The first four rounds of awards were organised by the Petroleum Division of the Ministry of Fuel and Power, headed from 1964 to 1972 by an unheralded but far-seeing civil servant, J. Angus Beckett, who curiously had also been a pioneer of Icelandic exploration, about which he wrote a rare and classic book, *Iceland Adventure*, in 1934. Beckett devised the methodology which governed the early years of exploration on the United Kingdom Continental Shelf, for which he was assailed by the Public Accounts Committee (chaired by Harold Lever) in 1973 for effectively handing out the North Sea licences on a plate, but Beckett fought back and was indeed vindicated. By adopting his policy of light work commitment and by favouring the so-called process of farming out (by which company A, having secured the licence, brought in company B to cover the drilling costs) the North Sea was explored rapidly and with immense benefit to the nation.

The reputation of the British civil service

and in particular of Beckett for absolute integrity was a key factor in the enthusiastic international response: dozens of American and Canadian companies applied, and then rose to the challenges both financial and engineering. It was Beckett's view that the North Sea licences, although dominated by the majors, should reflect a mix of the large, the medium-sized and the small or independent companies, and it is to Beckett's credit that the first North Sea oil field to be brought into production was by neither a major or a medium, but rather by an independent company, Hamilton Brothers, using a revolutionary floating technology. This was the Argyll Field. This was also an example of Beckett's determination to involve British non-oil companies and reach a benchmark of UK participation of no less than thirty per cent of the whole of the licensed areas. British companies as far removed from oil as United Biscuits, P&O and various banks had the wisdom and the courage to join in, mostly with American operating partners. In Hamilton's case their preferred partner was Associated Newspapers, at that time chaired by Esmond, the 2nd Viscount Rothermere. He had no cause to regret this joint venture – quite the reverse, as the Associated Newspaper share of the Argyll

Field cash flow must have been manna from the sea, enabling much-needed subsequent investment in newspaper technology.

The other conspicuous beneficiary of the Beckett formula was undeniably the City of London. Insurance companies, the banks and the stockbrokers have all played an important and creative part in the forty years since oil was discovered in the British sector of the North Sea. It was the stockbrokers and the more entrepreneurial banks that led the way. In a sense, initially they had been frustrated to discover how few, if any, senior executives left cosy positions within BP and Shell to raise funds to start their own new exploration companies (I was fortunate to secure the support of Barings Bank, which became a successful investment for them). Why these executives were so shy of leaving the security of BP and Shell we shall never know, but the London stockbrokers did not have long to wait before a stampede of junior American companies descended on London, and in many cases highly rewarding associations resulted, be they financings, joint ventures or the listing of new companies in London. Pre-eminent amongst these arrangements was Cazenove's relationship with Ranger Oil's Jack

Pierce, which was initiated and developed by a hardworking and certainly hard-drinking partner, Michael Belmont, whose colleagues had the sense to realise that he was in his element and gave him the support he needed. Alas, work and the alcohol eventually overwhelmed him, but not before Ranger and Cazenove had put together London and Scottish Marine Oil (LASMO), entirely funded by City institutions; it was a great North Sea success story.

Morgan Grenfell, Lazard's and Rothschilds all played a prominent role in funding North Sea development, in some cases with highly original financing geared to the special requirements of the widely differing oil companies. Another highly successful outcome of the Beckett formula was the Occidental Petroleum joint venture with Canadian-British Thomson organisation, owners then of *The Times* newspaper. If North Sea oil was squandered politically, as some suggest, it certainly had a dramatic role to play in reviving many struggling existing British companies. As I have said, the North Sea saga is now nearly fifty years old and many forecast another fifty years, primarily of gas production. Professor Peter Odell was the scourge of the oil companies in the 1970s and 1980s when he argued that they seldom operated in the interests of the country but tended to 'cream off' the easier reserves. The oil companies were indignant, but it does seem that over the years smaller discoveries had been made which the larger companies had then sat on, not judging them profitable enough for their purposes. The civil servants got wise to this and insisted on a policy of relinquishment; accordingly, contained in the current 33rd licensing round there are offered existing 'marginal' discoveries as well as pure exploration licences. Whereas in most parts of the world exploration rights are sold to their highest bidder and accordingly cost many millions of dollars, the UK system, again as devised by Angus Beckett, is known as a discretionary process: the government determines whether the applicant is a suitable company to own a licence by reason of the company's ability to 'tick' the appropriate boxes and attaches various levels of work commitment to the licence, rather than demanding a cash premium bonus. I regard this as a sensible policy as it renders the North Sea as a whole an attractive destination, particularly for the more adept and adroit entrepreneurs intent on farming out their acreage.

There are two purely political aspects of

North Sea policy I recall, the first being the Tory assumption that because the subject is fundamentally one of economics and business they know it all and require no advice. The second, characterised primarily by Cameron's term in office, has been the almost frantic game of musical chairs played by the Prime Minister with Ministers of State, to the extent that they seldom lasted more than an average of six months, not enough to make any impact and are accordingly all forgotten. I would, however, single out various Secretaries of State both Labour and Conservative for special mention. The most doctrinaire and controversial of these was far and away Anthony Wedgwood Benn, who with his left-leaning team, which included the Chairman of Courtaulds, Frank Kearton, and the Chief Executive of Guinness, Alastair Morton (who later ironically became Lady Thatcher's Gauleiter of choice as Chairman of the Eurotunnel) inflicted on the North Sea operators a period of doctrinaire challenge (or the largest waste of executive time since the last war – depending on whom you were talking to). This was the construction of the British National Oil Corporation (BNOC) to 'monitor' the activities of the oil companies through what became known as 'participation'. This was a Kafkaesque procedure, which stopped short of nationalisation but led to the appointment of BNOC representatives to sit on the crucial operating committees that managed the development and production of the various oil and gas fields. I recall observing at the time that this was analogous to the Escaping Committee at Colditz inviting the Camp Commandant to attend their deliberations! BNOC scarcely endeared itself to the North Sea companies by conducting the so-called participation negotiations in a high-handed and coercive manner. Meetings often began at 6pm and deliberately continued all night. There was widespread relief when Mrs Thatcher abolished it. It was certainly embarrassing and humiliating to be negotiating with astonished American partners *against* our own Government, which was conducting proceedings in such a maladroit fashion.

Two other Labour ministers were in sharp contrast to the belligerent Benn – namely Dr Dickson Mabon and Eric Varley, both alas deceased. Both were thoughtful, pragmatic and courteous. Equally, the prominent Conservative Ministers included David Howell, cerebral, wise and approachable, and Tom King, an affable and competent minister possessed of common sense.

As far as the individuals working for the companies are concerned, my closest connections beyond my own company were with BP. Most of the BP people were thoroughly decent lifelong executives, who were rewarded because of North Sea success with a sprinkling of CBEs and OBEs, but very seldom anything of a higher order except in the case of the Chairman, who was knighted almost without exception. A number of senior executives prominent in the North Sea saga had distinguished themselves as soldiers in the last war and held the DSO and/ or the MC. Of the senior management only Basil Butler of BP now survives, aged ninety-three. Others included Jack Birks, Monty Pennell and Sir Christophor Laidlaw (father of Sam, former Chief Executive of Centrica, now Executive Chairman of Neptune Oil).

But these BP executives had to deal with the turmoil created by the wave of nationalisations in the 1960s and 1970s, ranging from Saudi Arabia, Iran and Venezuela to Libya and Nigeria. However, the bonus for BP and others was the re-deployment of a cadre of young, experienced staff who knew how to get things done. In short, they didn't know what they were allowed to do, so they just did it without prior permission. True entrepreneurs.

This included the geologists, who shared a common belief in working as a team and enjoying a peripatetic, exciting lifestyle. Famous names include Norman Falcon, Peter Kent, John Martin, Terry Adams and Roger Herrera.

Peter Kent and his team quickly realised the impact of the discovery of gas at Groningen in the Netherlands, which dwarfed all existing discoveries and literally changed the energy map of north-west Europe. BP launched a marine seismic campaign in the southern North Sea in the early 1960s, led by a charismatic geophysicist named Jim Hornabrook. Using fairly primitive seismic technology, Hornabrook discovered the West Sole gas field in Block 48/6, and started production in 1967, opening a new chapter in the UK's energy security; crucially this came in advance of the times when Arthur Scargill's miners' union inflicted the 'three-day week', caused by shortage of coal for power generation.

Hornabrook's team extended the seismic exploration campaign to the central and northern North Sea and applied for Blocks 21/9 and 21/10 on a south-easterly trending feature, which they thought might become a drillable structure with more seismic. In fact, the feature was a huge Palaeocene submarine channel system which was the Forties oil field, eventually discovered by drilling in 1969.

Kent and Hornabrook's counterparts at Shell were led by Ken Glennie. Shell had applied for Block 22/6 – east of and adjacent to 21/10. Years later the Nelson oil field was discovered in 22/6. But it was really part of Forties.

Ken Glennie joined Shell in 1954 – and so began his worldwide travels. The principles of petroleum geology had only just begun to be formulated in the industry – as he famously said 'we had no idea where oil came from. Oil was where you found it; it just happened.'

Alaska

While all this was going on in the North Sea, BP opened an office in New York and sent a few geologists there. This was prompted by a federal lease sale in Alaska, a state which joined the Union only in 1958 as a state and was a magnet for gold, mineral and petroleum exploration. Roger Herrera and his team surveyed the Brooks Mountain Range with their United States Geological Survey (USGS) counterparts and quickly realised all the components for 'big oil' existed on the North Slope. As a result, BP applied for leases on half of what became the

Prudhoe Bay oil field – at more than 10 billion barrels the biggest oil field in the USA.

But the cost of developing two huge projects at the same time forced BP's debts up and share price down, resulting in a corporate crisis and changes in top management. Robert Horton left as CEO and David Simon took over to steady the ship.

The next generation of explorers included another cadre of outstanding geoscientists, engineers, lawyers and commercial specialists who learned their trade in the North Sea in the 1970s and 1980s, before putting BP's 'frontier exploration' strategy into practice all over the world in the 1990s.

This proved to be an enormous success, with huge benefits to host countries such as Angola, Colombia, Azerbaijan and Iraq. In exploration, BP and its partners discovered the Shah Deniz gas field in the Caspian Sea – BP's biggest ever operated discovery.

But BP exploration was virtually closed down two years ago on account of the environmental sensitivities associated with climate change. So, we are now left in a dilemma. We have British territorial waters containing the strong possibility of substantial new gas discoveries, maybe sustaining our energy security for another forty years. Should we not exploit these reserves rather than import, for example, liquefied natural gas from the Middle East? The North Sea episode has been one of the most remarkable events in our island history. We have not only earned a massive dividend from it, but we have learned so much too.

Perhaps overlooked is that Britain's ingenuity and capability to provide energy – not just oil and gas, but now wind and small nuclear – has evolved from the pioneering efforts by our people in the North Sea.

I contend that we should nurture this force for wealth and security with which we are blessed.

Then, Now and What Next?

To have been brought up in England in the 1940s and 1950s renders it rather bewildering to contemplate life in 2023. I do not know why or how I developed a strong sense of humour, particularly as I was an only child, and a very spoiled one at that. But it is at a time when there is not much to laugh about that laughter is so important. I certainly recall in the Army that, the bleaker the circumstances, the more we laughed, even on occasions laughing so much that it actually hurt. Richard Boston, the author, with whom

I shared a study at Stowe, edited the collected writings of Sir Thomas Urquhart, who actually died laughing; I have done my best during the successive seventy years to follow his example.

Why has humour become so unacceptable to so many, and why has it degenerated in quality to become so boorish, sexually crude, indeed so unfunny? After all, we have – so far – avoided being led by a dictator. Partially because our humour was so well developed that people devoid of humour but possessed of self-importance and pomposity were quickly exposed and expelled. A sense of humour projects a sense of the ridiculous, which is why a Hitler or Mussolini never secured power here. Those 20th-century politicians such as Curzon and Cripps never had a hope. The wit of F. E. Smith or the understatement of Clement Attlee were more to our taste.

I have always admired the precision with which Attlee dealt with bores and bullies. Crossman, being both of those, returned from a visit to Israel shortly after the war, brimming with Zionist zeal. He drove straight from London Airport to 10 Downing St and caught the Prime Minister, Attlee, alone, puffing at his pipe in the Cabinet Room. He unleashed a torrent of Zionist propaganda on the Prime

Minister for fully twenty minutes. When the flow ceased, Attlee took his pipe out of his mouth. 'How's your mother, Dick?' he said.

Another occasion was related to me by Paul Johnson. Paul attended the party given to launch Attlee's autobiography. He bought a copy and advanced on the distinguished old man and asked him if he would be good enough to sign it. Attlee accepted the book, took a pen out of his pocket and retreated into the corner and opened the book. Fully five minutes elapsed whilst Paul imagined the great man was composing an elegant dedication, perhaps in Latin. Finally, the pen began to move. Attlee closed the book and handed it back to Johnson, who thought it might be discourteous to open and read a dedication that had involved so much thought in front of Attlee. So he hailed a taxi and promptly opened the book. Attlee had inscribed the word 'Attlee' on the title page!

Humour was a natural characteristic neither of the left nor the right, whereas now its very existence is in jeopardy. I had lunch at the Old Bailey recently, and the distinguished judge whom I sat next to reported that judicial jokes are no more. Indeed, since they foolishly invited a well-known female *Guardian* columnist to lunch, neither are they allowed to drink (this embargo even extends to their guests), as she broadcast in the *Guardian* how outrageous it was to allow our overworked judges a gin and tonic. This is the same newspaper which caricatures the ex-governor of the BBC, Richard Sharp, in a cartoon vile in content. During my long life, I do not recall anything quite so unpleasant presented as a cartoon, which is identified by the *OED* as 'an amusing drawing'.

One of the primary pleasures of my life has been to read the wit of, for example, Cyril Connolly's James Bond parody *Bond Strikes Camp*. Or the diaries and letters of Evelyn Waugh. A laugh in every line – caustic, perhaps, but very funny indeed and not malicious. P. G. Wodehouse, the Master as he was known by his peers, Orwell and Waugh continue to provide an escape into that world that never existed, according to Waugh (although Wodehouse protested that indeed it had existed). No matter, a novel by Wodehouse is as necessary an ingredient in a civilised house as a bath or a bed. Now Penguin seeks to edit them to expunge offensive content. Offensive to whom?

I consider those who have a sense of humour and accordingly a sense of the ridiculous to be blessed in much the same way as people who enjoy the pleasure of reading are blessed.

My wife and I have three sons, all thankfully blessed with that all-important sense. If we have given nothing else, we have fulfilled a critical duty.

Where humour flags and dies then arrive the real tyrants and fascists, with their phoney solutions and grim prophecies. I believe that the source of all the problems of the world lies in uniformity. When localised culture dies, people naturally turn to something that can render them different from the herd. That uniformity is sinister – it binds us all into one market. You fly from Aberdeen to New Zealand and, when you arrive, you may just as well have not bothered. Everyone is wearing the same clothes. Everyone is listening to the same music and celebrating the latest art confidence trick. The present trans phase is a reflection of a desperate attempt *not* to be like everyone else. Self-importance is another sign of inadequacy.

In another sphere, the intellectual sterility of much environmental campaigning is frightening. Rather than a pipe-dream of net zero, we should be preparing for the worst and locking down our own energy security. Populists like Sturgeon and Starmer have no understanding of these issues.

There is little point in getting up in the

morning unless you are of an optimistic bent. However, confronted as one is with, for example, our current patronising, pompous and too-powerful London Mayor, that priceless sense of humour has to do a lot of heavy lifting. There needs to be a passionate fightback of common sense against the bores and the bullies.

Envoi

I WRITE THESE books with a fountain pen in capital letters at my desk with my back to the sea (on which there are constant distractions). The desk is in my study, which has been my study for just over fifty years. The room contains my favourite reference books. Wherever possible I abjure the use of the internet and favour my old friendly books, ranging from dictionaries of slang, of Australian colloquialisms, National Biography, *Chambers English Dictionary* (1901), *Concise Oxford* (1976) of which I have three copies (in the study, the dining room and my bedroom). My library is divided into sections as follows: Africa, Borneo, Burma, Malaysia, Hong Kong, Ceylon, Morocco, China, the sea, crime, P. G. Wodehouse, war and sport.

This library is the perfect companion as it can cope with my varying moods and can transfer me to my favourite places, put me together with my favourite people whilst always maintaining a float of as yet unread books. It scarcely contains a single novel written after 1950. I miss it when I am not in it and yearn to return to it. The time may not be so far distant when I shall not be able to leave it -- well, so be it. With the sea two hundred yards away, and surrounded by my books and hopefully by grandchildren, I may indeed be fortunate.

ACKNOWLEDGEMENTS

Harry Mount for his generous introduction, David Hooper (for advice on libel which has further reduced the length of this slim volume) and to my friends Philip Sidney, Sir Lloyd Dorfman, Derek Strauss, The Rt Hon. Michael Howard, A. N. Wilson, Robin Birley, Roger Seelig, Michael Bilbo and Peter Cowley for their advice on content. The opinions expressed are mine alone.

An Interview with the
Antiques Trade Gazette

ATG: How did you get the collecting bug?

Algy Cluff: There are two prongs to my collecting: I am the honorary librarian of The Royal Yacht Squadron so I collect for them. But I buy for myself too.

I bought my first pictures in 1957: six hand-coloured pictures of the Peninsular War (1807–14) by W. Heath (1795–1840). I bought them in Chester, and I still have them in my study. My first oil painting was a marine picture painted on slate by Thomas Luny (1759–1837).

I had no coherent plan for a collection. My father used to collect, and he was in wine shipping and bought only pictures of people drinking. But I do have one rule: I only buy pictures that either have a nude, a palm tree or a moon in them, and preferably all three. I like pictures depicting Africa and the Far East and I like the Daniells (Thomas, 1749–1840, William, 1769–1837, and Samuel, 1775–1811), in particular pictures of Oman and India.

In terms of books, I have been buying since I was fifteen. I like books from the 19th century up until the Second World War. I very much like crime novels written between 1920s–50s – you know the type, a dead body in the library and no sex.

I like Freeman Wills Crofts, who was a railway engineer and wrote in the 1940s–50s. I also collect anything about war and biographies and autobiographies of military figures, and I love books on the Far East and Africa.

The only novels I read are by P. G. Wodehouse and Evelyn Waugh. Contemporary fiction is so miserable.

Do you ever sell any of your collection?

I have sold things to improve my collection and to pay the tax man occasionally. But I don't buy to sell.

If I can buy another better condition copy of a book I have then I may sell one.

Why do you collect books?

Books become old friends. Not only are they a mental stimulus but they lend a great character to a room.

Interior designers don't seem to understand that. You hardly ever see a book in the rooms of glossy magazines.

I do have some sentimentality with books and especially the lower-value ones – I like to write my name and when I bought it.

Books are also great because burglars tend not to steal them.

Your library at home should contain books you haven't read. You should be able to go there and it be full of surprises, something you haven't read yet.

Another virtue of collecting books is that you can stumble across something wonderful for very little money. It's the thrill of the chase. You can't really do that with furniture or other items often.

How much do you typically spend?

I frequently buy books for around £100 but I probably wouldn't pay more than £500.

For paintings you can build a great collection spending less than £5,000 a picture.

Where do you buy?

I mourn the passing of Christie's South

Kensington. I bought so much there. There of course are other places and I also go to Bonhams in Knightsbridge and Chiswick Auctions. But I do miss Christie's. I thought it was an unfortunate business decision.

There are fewer bookshops than there were too. Of course, they are online, but I love to browse and see the books. I like Marrin's (Folkestone, Kent), and Adrian Harrington Rare Books (Tunbridge Wells). In London there is Heywood Hill (Curzon Street), John Sandoe (Chelsea) – these are both outstanding rare bookshops.

What do you expect to happen to your collections in the future?

I am lucky that all three of my sons read and love books. They don't spend all their time looking at screens. They are widely read: one is an expert on T. S. Eliot and my middle son Philip wrote a book on António de Oliveira Salazar. Our house is full of books, not just mine.

What is one thing we don't know about your collection?

I have four oil paintings of myself – one for each of my children and a spare. You can't get away from me in my house.

Now you have retired from your career in oil, gas and mining, how are you spending your time?

I am writing and promoting my books: *Get On With It, Unsung Heroes… And a Few Villains, By the Way…, Off the Cluff.*

I am Chairman and founder of The Remembrance Trust. I set it up to find, and where possible restore, the monuments and graves of military personnel worldwide of those killed prior to 1914. The Commonwealth War Graves Commission takes care of graves only from 1914 onwards. There is no one organisation that takes responsibility for graves and memorials before this date.

I recently donated one of the pictures from my collection to the charity: a portrait of Field Marshal Jan Christiaan Smuts.

This article was first published in *Antiques Trade Gazette* in May 2019. Reproduced with permission.

INDEX

Algy Cluff

Off the Cluff

Algy Cluff

By the Way...

From the Foreword to *By the Way...*
by Charles Moore

'Algy is a great reader, and has a lovely, economical literary style, but he writes chiefly about characters unknown to the world of letters. They emerge fresh from these pages…

'In his writing, he is himself a great memorialist of unusual customs, places and people – sharp, yet kind; sad, yet funny; modest, unique.'

Algy Cluff

Unsung Heroes

... and a few villains

FOREWORD BY
Simon Heffer

Algy Cluff

Get On With It

A Memoir

FOREWORD BY
A. N. Wilson

From the Foreword to *Get On With It*
by A. N. Wilson

'There's nothing worth the wear of winning,
But laughter and the love of friends'

'Algy's life bears this out. This book is the opposite of a misery memoir. It rejoices in his kind parents, his good friends and his happy marriage with three splendid sons. His boldness in the field of business and his merriment as a companion have their reward.'